MW00941286

CONDITIONING MANUAL

JIU JITSU

DEFENSE

A quick and easy way to learn method of
defense to match and surpass the toughness
of our enemies.

Published by

GORDY PUBLISHING COMPANY

CHICAGO, ILLINOIS

FOR VICTORY
BUY
UNITED
STATES
WAR
BONDS

UNITED STATES MARINE CORPS
MARINE AVIATION DETACHMENT
NAVAL TRAINING SCHOOL (AVIATION)
NAVY PIER, CHICAGO, ILL.

Seldom before in American history has it been so necessary for the young men of America to be well trained in the science of physical fitness and combat conditioning. War today creates demands that were never before thought possible.

The armies of our enemies have been trained for years to prepare them for the struggle that they alone knew was coming - the struggle for which they alone are responsible. Make no mistake about it, they are tough.

America's problem today is to match and surpass the toughness of our enemies - and this can be done only through a thorough and far reaching program of physical training.

Our young men have the physical ability to adapt themselves for modern warfare through their training in High School and College of such sports as Football, Basket Ball, Wrestling and Boxing.

The Marine Corps recognize this fact, and are giving more complete combat conditioning to their members than ever before. But before America's program of physical training can be complete, every able man should give himself the training that helps to build a strong body and the ability to defend one's self in physical combat.

LIEUT. COL. R. E. (DICK) HANLEY

United States Marine Corps Reserve
Officer-in-charge, Combat Conditioning.

Lieutenant-Colonel R. E. Hanley Reviewing Combat

Conditioning Practice

BOOK'S PURPOSE

In instructing the science of self-defense to various groups of Marines, it was discovered that there was a pressing need for some sort of basic reference guide for students to use as a "memory refresher" between classes. This book is the answer.

Since it was first printed as a pocket reference guide for Marine students of Jiu Jitsu Defense there have been innumerable requests for a third edition available to the general public. And because today as never before the knowledge of self-defense in physical combat is a necessary part of every man's makeup, these requests have been granted.

With more and more men being called into Uncle Sam's Armed Forces daily, the burden of protecting the home folks is doubly great for those of us left behind. For this reason, every able man owes it to America's loved ones to equip himself with the ability to give protection when the unforseen emergency arrives. Careful study of the methods described on the pages to follow will provide YOU with that ability.

Remember one thing—this book was not written to teach you a group of "tricks" to amuse your friends. Because only serious injury, or even death, can result from the forceful application of many of the holds it illustrates and teaches. In other words, this book was created only to help men when they're "fighting for keeps."

Copyright 1943

GORDY SERVICE CO.
Printers—Publishers
58 E. 18th St.
Chicago, Ill.

CONTENTS

PREPARING FOR JIU JITSU
DEFENSE FALLS AND THROWS

It is important to prepare the body for Jiu Jitsu slams.

After a little practice you will be able to throw and be thrown practically from any position without shock or injury to the body.

It is very important to exercise as shown on the following pages.

This will give you an idea on how to prepare for falls. Be sure to relax. When throwing an opponent in practice, grasp his sleeve near the muscle and hold him back slightly. Use either hand.

JIU JITSU DEFENSE FALLING
EXERCISE

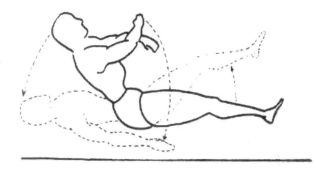

JIU JITSU FALLING EXERCISES

1. Lay flat, feet stretched out, chin pulled in, cross extended arms across chest and let them fall on mat in a slapping position, about 45° from body. Cup hands slightly. Repeat this many times.

2. Sit up, cross arms and fall back. Hand should slap mat at same time back does.

3. (Not sketched.) Lay flat on mat, cross arms. Rotate body to the left. The left arm then slaps the mat 45° from body. The right leg swings across the left leg, slapping the mat with the sole of the foot. Same movement for the right. Repeat this many times.

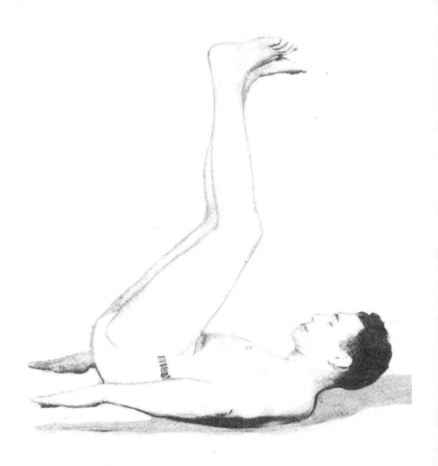

JIU JITSU DEFENSE FALLING
EXERCISE

1. Lay flat, feet stretched out, chin pulled in, cross extended arms across chest and let them fall on mat in a slapping position, about 45 degrees from body. Cup hands slightly. Repeat this many times.

2. Sit up, cross arms and fall back. Hand should slap mat at same time back does.

JIU JITSU DEFENSE FALLING
EXERCISE

FALLING EXERCISES

When you are thrown by an opponent with the hip throw or over-shoulder throw, twist your body while falling in same position as sketched. Your hand must be 45° from your body. Slap hard against mat at the moment of impact of your body.

JIU JITSU DEFENSE FALLING
EXERCISE

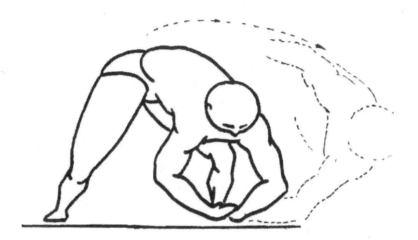

FALLING EXERCISES

In falling forward take 1 step forward. Your left foot will be extended, fingers pointing towards your body. Put your right hand on your left hand, palm down, fingers pointing toward your left hand. Your arms will then form a circle. Roll towards your left, rotating on your left arm, shoulder and back. Keep arms in a circular position. Then you will come up on your feet.

JIU JITSU FALLING EXERCISE

ACTION 1

In falling forward, your left foot must be extended, bend
down and place your left hand close to the mat, fingers
pointing to your right foot. Put your right hand on your
left hand, palm down, fingers pointing to your left. Your
arms will then form a circle.

JIU JITSU FALLING EXERCISE

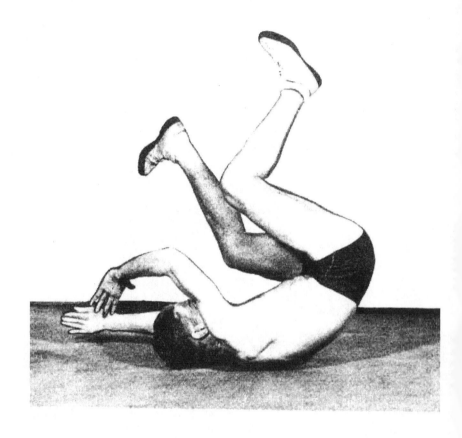

ACTION 2

Roll towards your left, rotating on your left arm, shoulder and back.

JIU JITSU FALLING EXERCISE

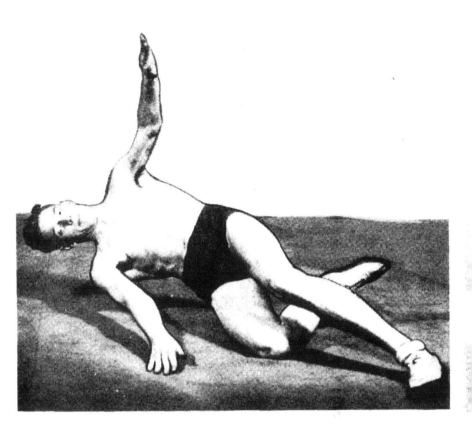

ACTION 3

When landing on mat, your right hand will be extended
45 degrees from your body, your left foot extending
over your slightly bent right foot.

JIU JITSU FALLING EXERCISE

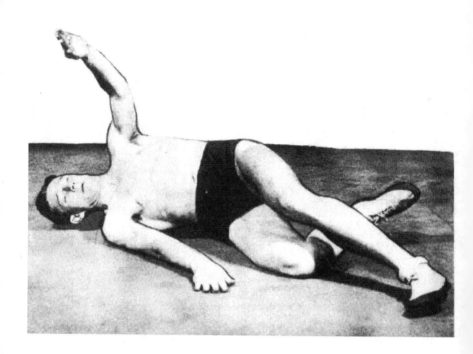

FINISH

Your right will slap the mat with your right hand slightly
cupped, at the same time your body lands.

WRIST THROW

The wrist break and throw is one of the first and important things that you must learn to be a successful Jiu Jitsu player.

As the first thing your enemy will do is to strike at you which exposes his hand for a wrist throw.

Most successful throws are when the palm is turned back and you apply plenty of leverage by pushing his arm back to the side. Very often you will grab a man's hand and attempt to force his wrist back and he will stiffen it so that you can't bend it, pretend that you are going to pull the arm towards you, he will then try and pull it back. Step right in and this motion will cause him to bend his own wrist. It is important that you use the same hand and the same foot in applying any wrist breaks.

ILLUSTRATING START AND FINISH
OF WRIST THROW

WRIST THROW

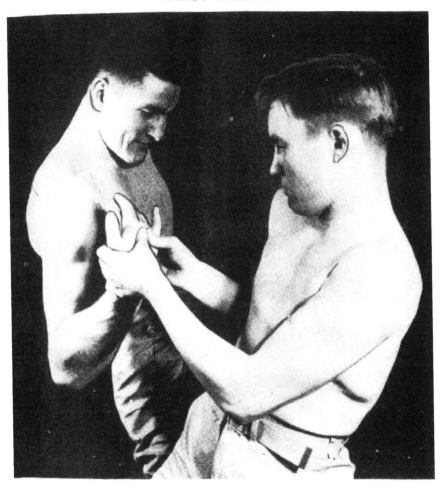

ACTION 1

Grasp opponent's right hand with your left hand palm facing down. Your fingers are curled around his thumb. Press your thumb hard against the back of opponent's hand. Raise his hand shoulder high applying your right hand in the same manner. Twist and push to your left and force his wrist backwards and down.

WRIST THROW

ACTION 2

Place your right foot against his right foot blocking it
from the back and throw him to the ground.

WRIST THROW

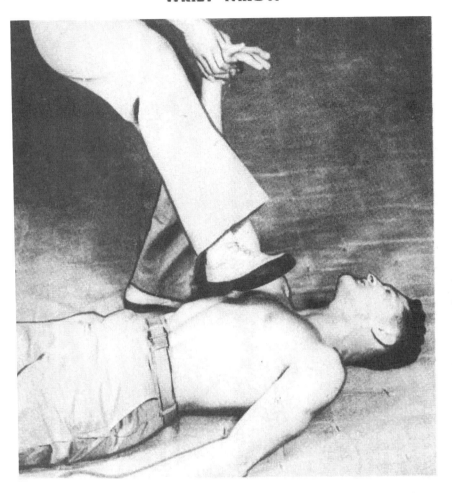

FINISH

Hold his right hand tightly and with the heel of your shoe stamp into head or testicles.

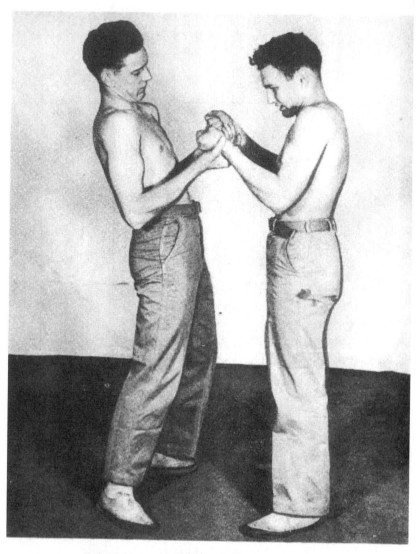

DOUBLE WRIST HOLD BREAK

Opponent grasps your wrists, standing directly in front of you with his thumbs up. To free yourself, press both of your elbows to your sides, step towards him at the same time, draw your hands in and up against your opponent's thumbs.

If your opponent is very powerful, press your arms down and against him, then bend your forearms sharply in, up and out.

ILLUSTRATING EDGE OF HAND SLASH

START

FINISH

EDGE OF HAND SLASH

CAUTION: These slashes are very dangerous.

Deliver slashing blow with arm slightly bent; fingers straight and close together. Palm of hand must face down. Strike either side of neck or spine close to head or to adams apple. Use either hand for slashing.

Extremely dangerous are slashes against the bridge or base of the nose.

VULNERABLE SPOTS FOR KNOCKOUT BLOWS

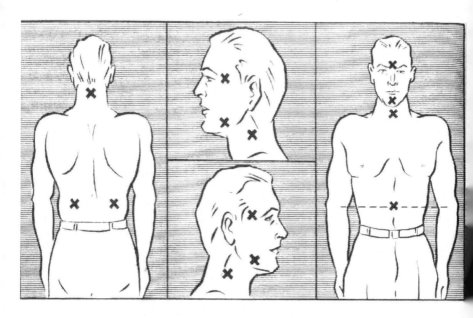

The spots illustrated herein are vital and blows striking against them will knock a man unconscious or kill him. It is best to use the edge of the hand slash against these spots.

KICK DEFENSE
AGAINST CLUB, KNIFE, BLOW

Pivot so as to be at right angles with the opponent. Clasp hands in front of chest to maintain balance. Kick leg straight out from hip, bringing foot back fast for additional kick. Aim at vulnerable spots, knee caps, testicles, heart, etc.

Use caution in practice.

KICK DEFENSE AGAINST SHARP WEAPONS

Enemy attempts to use knife, club, or fist. Step in as if you were going to box with him, grasping both hands directly in front of you for balance. Turn your foot at right angles from your enemy and kick hard, bringing the foot back immediately for another kick. Vulnerable spots are the knee-cap, testicles, stomach, heart or into the neck. This is a very important defense and a lot of practice is required, as the foot is used in the same manner as a fist would be. It must be shot quickly and returned immediately into position for another kick. Use caution in practice.

24

KICK DEFENSE AGAINST CLUB, BLOW

Pivot so as to be at right angles with the opponent. Clasp hands in front of chest to maintain balance. Kick leg straight out from hip, bringing foot back fast for additional kick. Aim at vulnerable spots, knee caps, testicles, heart, etc.

Use caution in practice.

KIDNEY BLOW AGAINST BOXER

Opponent is aiming a blow at your head with his right fist.

Side step to the left pushing his right elbow to his left with your left hand. Pivot to your right until your body is facing the same direction as his, and smash your left elbow into his ribs, kidneys, heart or testicles.

BREAK FOR BACK HUG UNDER ARMS

(Instructions on following page)

BREAK FOR BACK HUG UNDER ARMS

Opponent grasps you from around the waist from the back holding you tightly. Step forward with either foot and bend forward slightly. Clasp your hands shoulder high; swing hard to either side striking his head with your elbows.

Or:

Grind heel of your shoe into his toes or instep or reach back and grasp his testicles:

BACK HOLD, OVER ARMS BREAK
ACTION 1

Enemy grasps you from the back, locking your arms to your sides. Immediately step forward with your right foot, form a "V" by clasping your hands together, take a deep breath.

BACK HOLD, OVER ARMS BREAK
ACTION 2

Force your arms up, shoulder high, exhaling at the same
time. This will loosen his arms slightly.

BACK HOLD, OVER ARMS BREAK
FINISH

Bend down quickly while still clasping your hands, thus forming a pivot. Jab your left elbow into your opponent's heart, side, stomach or testicles. Use caution in practice.

DEFENSE FOR BACK HOLDS OVER ARMS

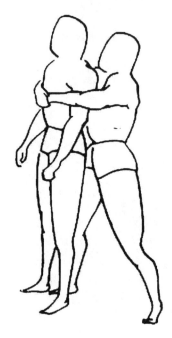

START

FINISH

(Instructions on opposite page)

DEFENSE FOR BACK HOLDS OVER ARMS

If enemy grabs you from the back locking your arms against your body step forward slightly with your right foot. Clasp your hands together and at the same time taking a deep breath, bring your hands up quickly and exhaling at the same time. Then with his hands loosened, grasp his right muscle with your left hand and with your right hand grasp him high near the collar and go into the "Over Shoulder Throw"

Or:

Jab your left elbow into his kidneys.

BREAK FOR FRONT HUG

(Instructions on opposite page)

FRONT HUG BREAK

ACTION 1

Your opponent grasps you tightly from the front, locking your arms to your sides. Place your hands flat against his thighs, forcing him to back away from you; or bite his ear, causing him to bend forward.

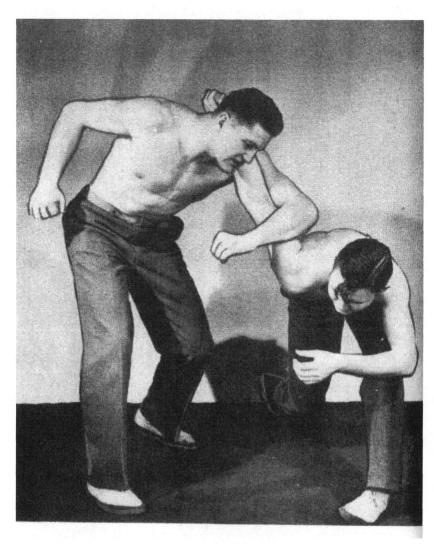

FRONT HUG BREAK
ACTION 2

You can also grasp his testicles, forcing him to step back, and with your left hand reach up and over in a circular movement, forcing his right arm against your neck and shoulder. Push down hard on his arm causing considerable pain, or break.

FRONT HUG BREAK
FINISH

When he lowers his head, you slash with your right hand against the back of his neck, or kick with knee into his chin.

BREAK FOR BACK HUG UNDER THE ARMS
FOOT GRAB

Opponent grasps you around the waist from the back, holding you tightly. Attempt to grab his hair, then suddenly bend forward, grasping his leg with both your hands. Pull forward and lean back, causing yourself to fall back on him and if your fall is hard you will injure him severely. Use caution in practice.

SLASH AT THROAT WITH KICK BACK

When attacked by enemy with a knife in his right hand, step to his left, slash your left hand into his windpipe. Grab his left hand at same time insert your left foot behind his left foot. Pull toward your right on his arm. Push back hard on his neck, causing him to take a very violent back fall. Kick into his heart, when he is down on ground. Either hand may be used. Very dangerous. Caution in practice.

SLASH AT THROAT WITH KICK BACK

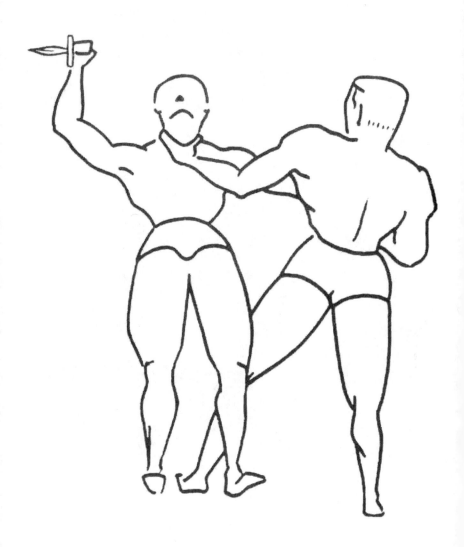

(Instructions on opposite page)

SLASH AT THROAT WITH KICK BACK

When attacked by enemy with a knife in his right hand, step to his left, slash your left hand into his windpipe. Grab his left hand, at same time insert your left foot behind his left foot. Pull toward your right on his arm. Push back hard on his neck, causing him to take a very violent back fall. Kick into his heart, when he is down on ground. Either hand may be used. Very dangerous. Caution in practice.

SHOULDER BREAK AGAINST KNIFE
START

Enemy attempts to jab you from the side with knife in
his right hand. Grasp his right wrist with your right
hand thumbs down; and with your left hand thumbs
down; push down on his arm then suddenly pull his
arm upwards.

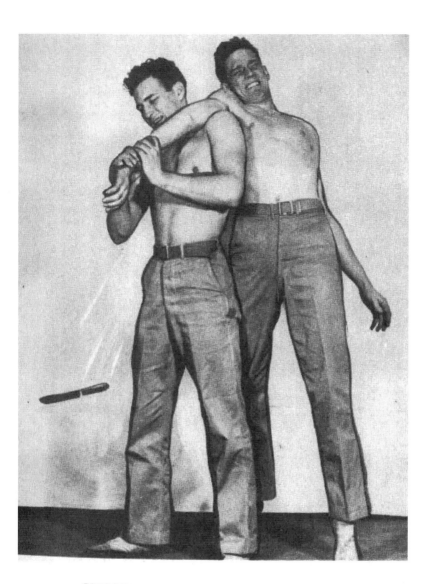

SHOULDER BREAK AGAINST KNIFE
FINISH

Bring your right foot behind you, bending down slightly which will face you in the same position as your opponent; force your left shoulder under his raised right arm; rotate his arm so that his hand is palm up. Pull down hard on his arm, pushing up on his shoulder. This will break and dislocate his arm and shoulder.

CHIN JAB AND KICK BACK

Enemy attempts to strike you with club in his right hand.
Step to his right side at the same time blocking the blow
with your left hand. Insert your right foot behind his
right foot, at the same time kick back and jab hard into
his chin with your open palm.

This is very dangerous as it will dislocate his neck and
throw him backward violently.

BREAK AGAINST ELBOW

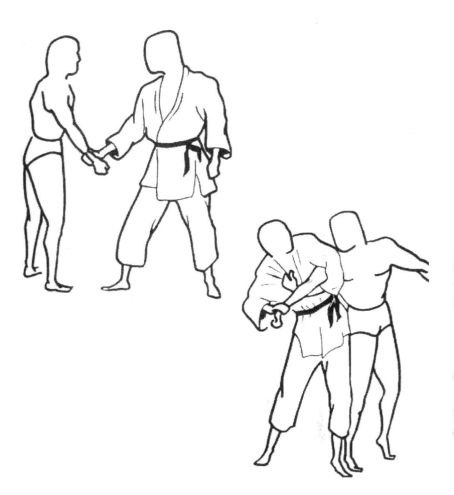

Enemy attempts to strike you with his right hand, grasp his right hand with your right hand. With your thumb up, pull him toward you slightly; his arm must be rotated palm up and at same time step behind him toward your left. You will then be facing the same way. Wrap your left arm around his right arm muscle tightly and grab your own coat lapel to your right. Push your hip into his and force his captured arm down with your right hand, thereby causing considerable pain or breaking the arm.

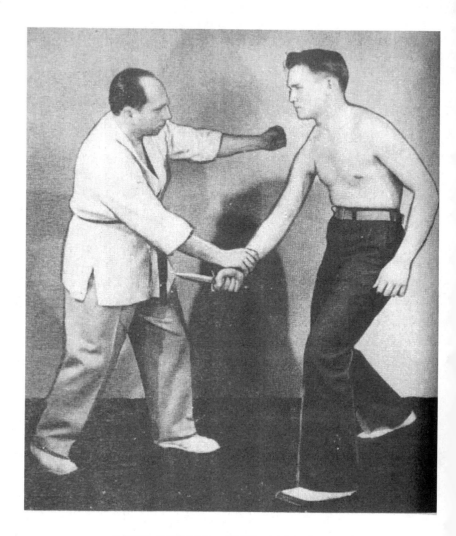

ARM BREAK, AND MARCHING
PRISONER HOLD
ACTION 1

Enemy attempts to stab you with an upward motion.
Grasp his right wrist with your right hand, thumb to
your left, at the same time pulling his arm down and
towards you and keeping him off balance.

ARM BREAK, AND MARCHING
PRISONER HOLD
ACTION 2

While continuing to hold his arm step back so that you
are then facing in the same direction as he. At the same
time slash with your left hand into his windpipe.

ARM BREAK, AND MARCHING
PRISONER HOLD
FINISH

Wrap your left arm around his right arm close to his shoulder. Grasp your own coat near the right collar. Lean back slightly, applying pressure against his shoulder and pull down on his captured arm, thereby causing such terrific pain as will make him drop his weapon. You can march your enemy by holding his arm in this position.

BREAK FOR FULL NELSON

Your opponent puts a full nelson on you from the back. This will force your neck down slightly and your arms up. Step to your right with your right foot and suddenly insert your left foot behind your opponent's right foot. Bend back from the hip, at the same time forcing your right arm against your opponent's face. If he holds on tightly he will cause you to fall backward on top of him. This is very dangerous, as you may fall hard into his stomach or chest and either knock him out or break his ribs, so use caution in practice.

FRONT TRIP AND ARM BREAK
ACTION 1

Enemy attempts to strike you with right fist. Grasp his
fist with your right hand, thumbs down, pull him towards
you; pivot towards your right so you are facing the way
he is; insert your left foot in front of him; your left toe
pointing towards your right; force his shoulder down with
your left hand; continue pulling with your right.

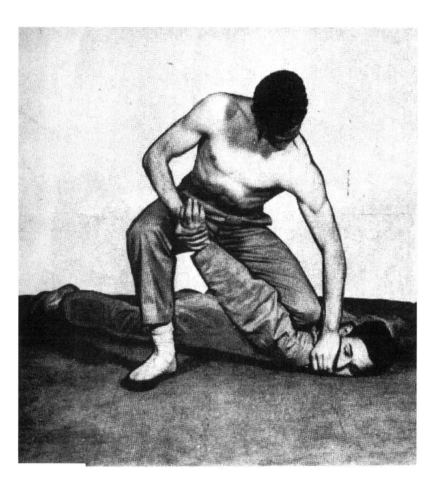

FRONT TRIP AND ARM BREAK
FINISH

While your opponent is falling forward over your left leg, continue holding his right hand; when he is flat on ground, force your knee against his right shoulder with your left leg; pull his extended arm up towards you which will cause dislocation.

For additional punishment, grasp his chin with your left hand and pull up violently.

This fall is very dangerous, use caution in practice.

SHOULDER PRESSURE ARM BREAK

(Instructions on opposite page.)

SHOULDER PRESSURE ARM BREAK

If opponent slides his right hand under your left arm pit capture it and break it by twisting your left arm around the outside of his while your right arm rests on his shoulder. Grasp your own right arm with your left hand and pull up with your left hand and lean back slightly. This will cause considerable pain or break his arm. This hold can be applied with either hand.

ACTION AGAINST ARM AND SHOULDER

Your opponent is directly in front of you; he attempts to strike a low blow with his right hand; block his right arm with your left hand slightly bent at the same time grasp his sleeve at the muscle with your right hand force his arm back with your left hand and at the same time rotating so that it is in the crotch of your arm and your left hand is now on his right muscle; force his bent arm up and across his back; lean towards him forcing him to bend forward with upward pressure of your left arm; to secure him grasp his collar with your right hand.

CROSSED ARM HOLD AND CHIN BLOW

Opponent attempts to strike you with his left hand. Step to your right clasp his wrist with your left hand, thumbs down, pulling him toward you slightly. Step forward with your right foot, at the same time wrapping your right arm around his left arm. Rotate his arm upwards and backwards as you clasp your own wrist with the thumb down. Force your elbow hard into his face and step behind him, using a kickback.

THROWS WITH THE HIP

Throwing with the hip is the commonest and most important of all throws. There is a lot of power in the hip when it is properly applied. Proper motion of the hip is to lower it slightly and rotate it backwards, quickly and upwards. The hip should be used in throwing when your opponent is standing still and resisting you. If you will follow instructions on the following pages, you will find the hip a very easy and effective means of throwing your opponent.

OVER-SHOULDER THROW

In the over-shoulder throw, your opponent is pushing you backward, you turn suddenly on him so you are facing the same direction as he is. In this case, you use your hips and shoulders combined in throwing your opponent.

STRAIGHT FOOT THROW

In this throw, you do not use your hip but your right foot and apply it only when your opponent is pushing backward.

FRONT HIP THROW

Grab your opponent's right arm at the muscle with your left hand, wrap your right arm around his waist, and turn forcing your right hip into his stomach. Lean forward to your left and pull down on his right arm—throwing him violently forward.

HIP THROW AND FALL
ACTION 1

Enemy attempts to grapple with you. Step into him;
throw right arm around his waist, close to his shoulder;
turn your body to your left so you are facing the same
direction he is, at the same time grasp his right sleeve
high up on his shoulder; insert your hip hard into his
stomach; bend down, pulling him toward you so that
your hip throws him forward violently.

HIP THROW AND FALL
ACTION 2

Your opponent will fall in this manner and if you are thrown with the same hold, you must learn to fall by keeping your left arm 45 degrees from your body and relaxing.

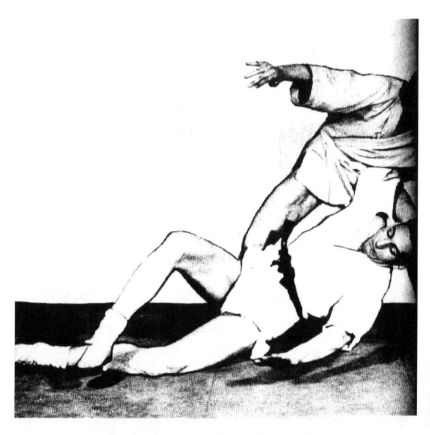

HIP THROW AND FALL
FINISH

Your whole body should strike the ground at the same
time. Your right leg is over your left in a bent position.
It should strike the ground at the same time your hand
does.

ANKLE THROW

Grasp your opponent's right lapel with your left hand, thumb up. At the same time grasp his left sleeve near the shoulder with your right hand. Spring in towards him on your right foot, at the same time laying your left ankle against his left ankle. Force your hip into his stomach and, in one motion, pull up with your left hand and down with your right, bending slightly towards your right and forcing your right ankle against his left ankle in a raising motion. Pull down with both hands and at the same time raise him with your ankle, causing him to take a very violent forward fall. This throw requires a great deal of practice, and is very dangerous.

BACK HIP THROW

(Instructions on opposite page)

BACK HIP THROW

CAUTION: This fall is very dangerous. Grasp your opponent's right arm at the muscle with your left hand. Step behind him with your right foot inserting your hip against the back of his. Grasp his left arm with your right hand and pull down with your left while bending your knees slightly; rotate hip upwards thus throwing him to the ground.

Finish: Hold on to his left arm tightly and while keeping him slightly off the ground kick down with the heel of your shoe into his heart or head.

STRAIGHT FOOT THROW

Enemy is choking you from the front.

Grab his right arm at the muscle with your left hand, thumb up and with your right hand grab his coat lapel. Step back until your left foot is back, his right foot will be forward. Put your weight on your left foot. Extend your right foot to the outside of his right ankle. Trip him with your right foot by pulling and leaning towards your left and push him backwards with your right hand. This will cause him to fall on his back.

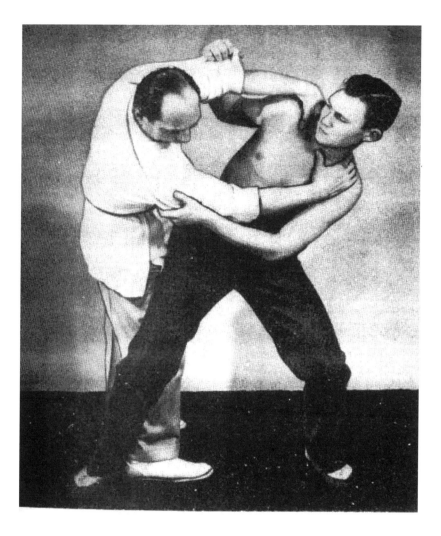

STRAIGHT FOOT THROW

Enemy is choking you from the front.

Grab his right arm at the muscle with your left hand, thumb up and with your right hand grab his left sleeve. Step back until your left foot is back, his right foot will be forward. Put your weight on your left foot. Extend your right foot to the outside of his right ankle. Trip him with your right foot by pulling and leaning towards your left and push him backwards with your right hand. This will cause him to fall on his back.

CIRCLE THROW

(START)

Grasp opponent by the collar or back of arms. Force him backwards slightly. He will then push against **you** forcing you backwards. You will then lean back while kicking him in the stomach with either foot and pulling him towards your face. While lying flat on your **back,** with bent foot kick hard straight up throwing your opponent over your head.

CIRCLE THROW
(FINISH)

The author is here demonstrating how to break a fall when thrown by "Circle Throw."

The fist comes down first and you roll on your arm rolling across your shoulder and slapping the mat hard just before your back lands.

OVER SHOULDER THROW

(Instructions on opposite page)

OVER SHOULDER THROW

If opponent attempts to choke you from behind with his right arm around your neck, step forward slightly with your right foot and at the same time grasp his arm at he elbow with your left hand. Reach up with your right hand grasping his clothes at his right shoulder. Stoop forward suddenly, and forcing your hips violently into his stomach, pull him over your shoulder.

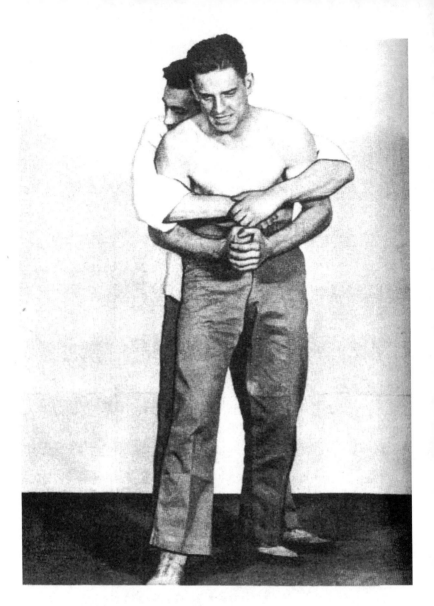

OVER SHOULDER THROW AND FALL
ACTION 1

Your opponent grasps you from behind, locking your arms to your side. Clasp your hands together and at the same time take one step forward with your right foot.

OVER SHOULDER THROW AND FALL
ACTION 2

Force your clasped hands up suddenly and at the same
time bend forward slightly. Reach up and grasp your
opponents right sleeve or arm with your right hand high
up on the shoulder and with your left hand grasp his
sleeve or arm at the muscle.

OVER SHOULDER THROW AND FALL
ACTION 3

Pull him down and forward against your hip and shoulder.
Insert your hip hard into your opponent's stomach. This
will throw him forward violently.

In practice, if you are falling, relax and slap mat with
your hand 45 degrees from your body.

OVER SHOULDER THROW AND FALL
FINISH

In throwing your opponent, you can break his right arm while he is falling by anchoring his right arm under your left arm pit, and placing both of your hands at his elbow. Lean back at the same time.

Use caution in practice.

CRAB CLAW THROW

This is used for disarming against a knife:

The action is done by grasping his right wrist with your left hand and resting your right on the ground and jumping against his body with your feet spread apart; your left foot high against his waist and your right against the the back of the ankles. Twist towards the left causing your opponent to take a very vicious fall.

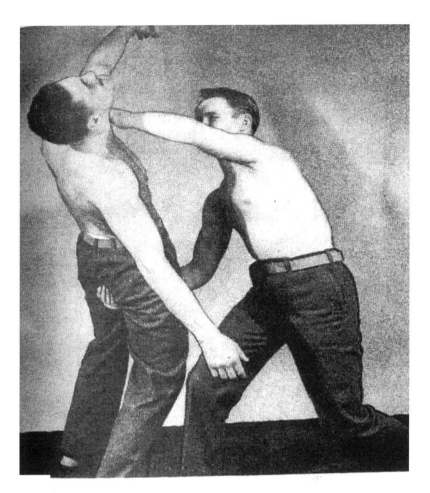

FRONT GRAB FOR BACK THROW, WITH
SLASH IN THROAT

Enemy attempts to grab you. Bend down quickly towards his right with your right foot extended. Slash at his throat with your left hand, which will cause him to bend back; at the same time insert your right hand between his legs, trying to grab his belt from the back, or the seat of his trousers. Pull forward with your right hand, forcing him backwards with your left-hand slash, and causing him to fall backwards. This fall is very dangerous and is very likely to kill your opponent. Be very careful in practice.

Reverse action for a front throw.

CHOKE BREAKS

The following pages consist of a variation of cnoke breaks. When an enemy attempts to choke you, the most important thing to remember in most cases not to grab for his hands that seem to be choking the life out of you. First in importance is the straight jab with the arm and fingers into the windpipe. The next is the slash into the throat from the side and then comes the V-thrust into the face or the pit of the stomach. Then the pull forward and kick the knee in the testicles. And then the arm breaks and the pull downs with kick of the knee into the face. These breaks are important and a good deal of time and practice should be used. Be very careful in practise as they are all very dangerous.

CHOKE BREAKS

CLASPED HAND THRUST

Clasp your hands forming a V. Thrust up hard against the arms and strike face with a downward movement; in so doing opponent's nose and face is smashed.

CHOKE BREAK

FINGER JAB IN THE THROAT

Enemy attempts to choke you:

Jab hand with fingers held rigid hard into opponent's windpipe. Either hand may be used. Take one step forward and thrust knee into testicles.

CHOKE BREAK
CLASPED HAND THRUST WITH KNEE KICK

Clasp your hands forming a V. Thrust up hard against the arms thus breaking the choke hold. Grasp him by the shoulders pulling him toward you. Then drive your knee into his testicles.

79

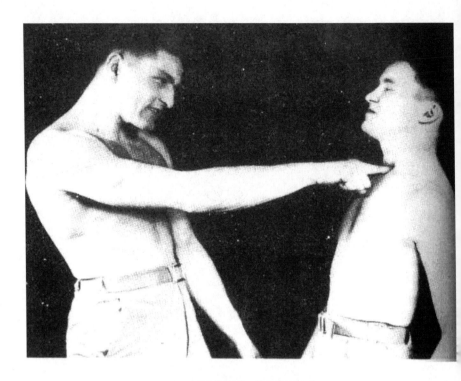

CHOKE BREAKS

Enemy attempts to choke you, or grab you. Force your forefinger into the lower windpipe, and push in with a rotating motion, forcing him to back away. Use slash to disable.

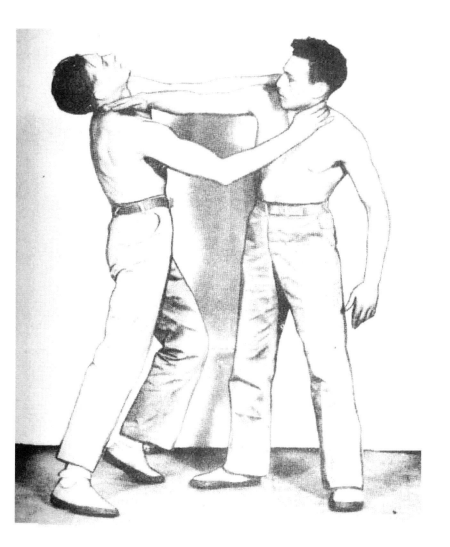

CHOKE BREAK WITH ARM SLASH

Enemy attemps to choke you from the front with both hands. Slash to the right side of his throat with your right hand. Your palm must be turned down. Use either hand. Very dangerous in practice.

CHOKE BREAK WITH JAE
INTO THE HEART

Enemy attempts to choke you from back or side, with both hands. Clasp both of your hands together forming a pivot; bend down slightly and jab your elbow into heart, stomach or testicles.

LEAN BACK ARM BREAK

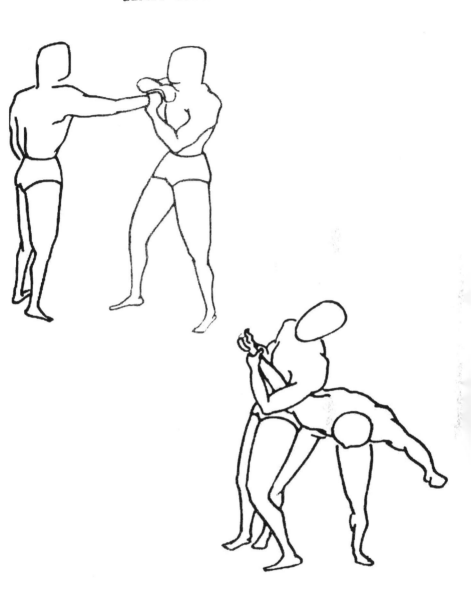

(Instructions on following Pages)

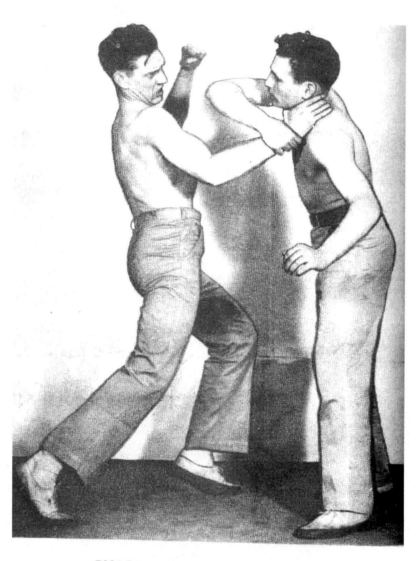

SINGLE ARM CHOKE BREAK
START

Enemy attempts to choke you with his right hand stand
ing directly in front of you. Grasp his wrist with your
right hand thumb down. Turn and bring your right foot
behind you. You will be facing the same direction as
he is. Continue holding on to his right hand pulling for
ward and downward slightly.

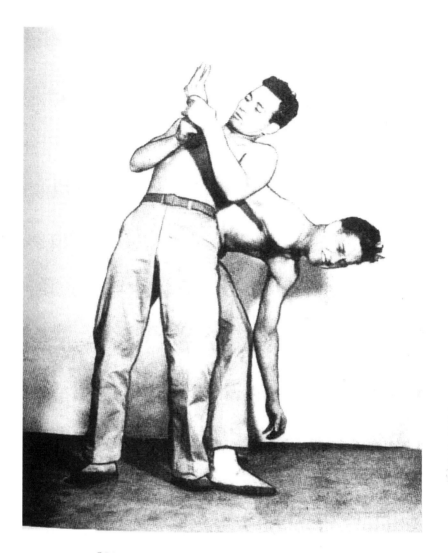

SINGLE ARM CHOKE BREAK
FINISH

Pull his arm under your left arm pit. His hand must be
rotated so his palm is up. Lean back and down hard
against his extended arm. This will cause it to break.
Use caution in practice.

COLLAR GRAB ARM BREAK
(START)

Enemy grabs the collar with his right hand. Grasp his right wrist with your right hand, thumbs down, and with your left hand on his wrist, also thumbs down. Force his hand against your shoulder.

COLLAR GRAB ARM BREAK
(FINISH)

Turn and bring your right foot behind you. You will be facing the same direction he is. Continue holding onto his right hand at the same time rotating it so that his palm is up. Lean back in a falling position against his arm while pulling up on wrist. By relaxing slightly and pulling down a little on his wrist and up suddenly his arm can be broken very easily.

BREAK FOR STRAIGHT ARM CHOKE

START

FINISH

(Instructions on following page)

FRONT CHOKE BREAK WITH
KNEE PRESSURE
ACTION 1

Enemy attempts to choke you with both hands standing directly in front of you. To break, move your left foot slightly towards the rear, cross your left hand over his right and grab his left wrist with your thumb down.

FRONT CHOKE BREAK WITH
KNEE PRESSURE
ACTION 2

Force the palm of your right hand against the back of his left elbow. Pull his arm straight by stepping back slightly. Continue downward pressure on his left elbow.

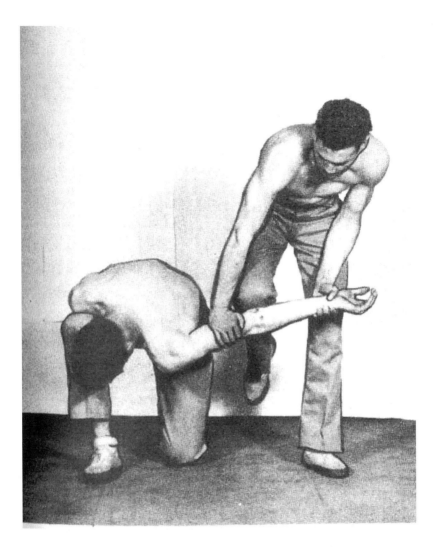

FRONT CHOKE BREAK WITH
KNEE PRESSURE

FINISH

Force your opponent downward until he is on his knee;
at the same time rotating his arm so that his palm is
facing upward and his thumb towards you. Pull up with
your left hand and push down with your right. For quick
break, force your right knee hard against his elbow.

CHOKE BREAK WITH KNEE KICK

Enemy attempts to choke from the front with both hands. Cross your hands over his bearing down quickly at the same time kicking your knee into his testicles or chin.

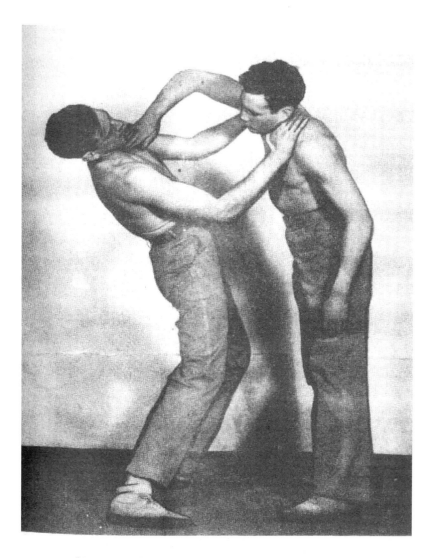

CHOKE BREAK JAB INTO THROAT

Enemy attempts to choke you with both hands from the front. Jab hard with either hand, fingers stiffened into your opponent's throat.

ARM LEVER BACK STRANGLE

(Instructions on following page)

ARM LEVER BACK-STRANGLE

Enemy attacks you with knife in his right hand:
Seize his right wrist with your right hand with your
thumb to the left. Turn so that you are behind enemy.
Extend your left leg behind him—wrap your left arm
around his neck from the front forcing his head back
at the same time pulling this right arm across your chest
thereby strangling him.

DOUBLE PRESSURE BACK-STRANGLE
START

Throw your right arm around opponent's neck from the
back; clasp your own right hand with your left, forcing
your opponent's head against your shoulder and head.

DOUBLE PRESSURE BACK-STRANGLE
FINISH

Force your opponent down in a sitting position so that
his back rests on your right knee. Pull back hard on
your right arm and push forward with your head and
right shoulder, thereby causing immediate strangulation.
Very dangerous.

(Instructions on opposite Page)

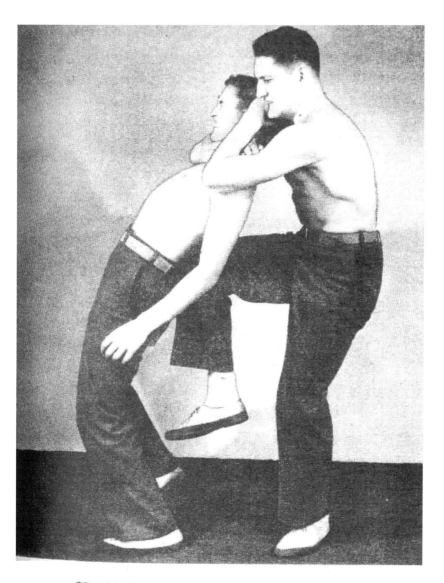

STRANGLE WITH KNEE IN BACK

Step behind opponent and clasp your right forearm against his windpipe pulling his head back slightly. Your left arm is extended over his left shoulder—grasp your left muscle with your right hand and push against the back of his head with the palm of your left hand. Insert your right knee into his back and bring him back slowly, strangling him.

WRAP AROUND CHOKE

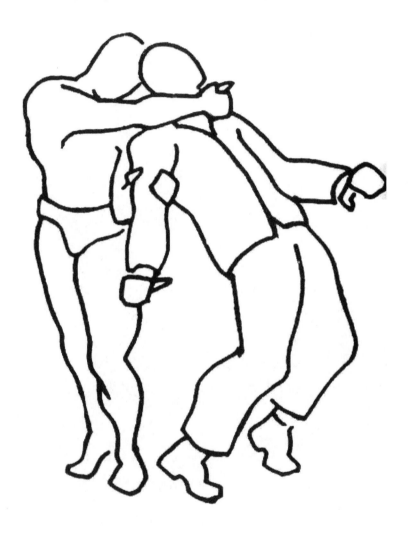

(Instructions on opposite Page)

WRAP-AROUND CHOKE

With your opponent directly in front of you reach out with right hand and grasp collar behind left ear — thumb down. Grab right arm back of muscle and pull him violently toward you and at the same time stepping directly behind him. Keep tight grasp of collar and your right forearm stiff against his windpipe. Then bend him back, and with your left hand grasp his left hand at the wrist so that his palm is facing out. Force his arm against your chest by pulling it backwards, and pull hard with your right arm against his windpipe causing strangulation.

WRAP AROUND CHOKE
ARM BREAK
START

With your opponent directly in front of you, reach out
with right hand and grasp collar behind left ear -- thumb
down. Grab right arm back of muscle and pull him
violently toward you and at the same time stepping
directly behind him. Keep tight grasp of collar and your
right forearm stiff against his windpipe. Then bend him
back and insert your left arm between his back and
left arm. Force your knuckles into his back.

WRAP AROUND CHOKE
ARM BREAK
FINISH

Pull back with your right arm at the same time forcing him to ground, face downwards. Now grasp his left wrist, pull back hard with your left hand. Continue pulling upwards with your right hand for quick strangle.

CROSSED ARM CHOKE WHEN
KNOCKED DOWN

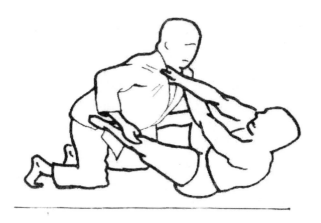

When you are knocked backwards or you miss a circle throw use a cross arm choke and push your feet into your opponent's stomach, raising your opponent slightly from the mat. This will force his neck hard into your crossed arms. Pull and twist hard on your arms and this will cause immediate strangulation. To counter this choke, slash your extended fingers and hand into his exposed throat or grab for his testicles.

This is very dangerous in practice. Use caution.

CHOKING OPPONENT WHEN KNOCKED DOWN

When attempting to choke an opponent, with crossed arm choke, when you are flat on your back, insert both of your legs in your opponent's stomach, raising him off the ground. This will cause him to fall forward and strangle himself. To counter this choke, jab extended finger into throat.

CHOKING OPPONENT IF YOU
MISS A CIRCLE THROW

When attempting to use a cross arm choke, and circle throw, and if you miss the throw, let him fall between your legs and immediately apply a scissors hold and continue choking.

To counter this choke, grab his testicles or apply your elbows in a rotating manner to his thighs.

SPINE BREAK PRESSURE HOLD

To capture enemy, step in close facing him directly.
Throw your right arm around his neck, step to the left
with your right foot so that his body is directly behind
yours. Slide him onto your back with a hip movement to
your right, lowering your body at the same time. Wrap
your left arm around his left leg. He is then directly
across your back. Grasp the inside of your thighs with
both hands, thumbs up. Hold on to your thighs and, to
apply pressure, bring your legs together. This will
eliminate or crush your enemy in a few minutes.

ILLUSTRATING DEFENSE AGAINST KNIFE
WHEN KNOCKED DOWN

START

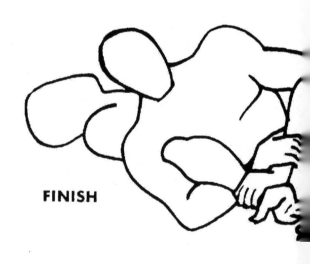

FINISH

(Instruction on next page)

DEFENSE AGAINST KNIFE
WHEN KNOCKED DOWN

You are knocked flat on your back—

Enemy is holding you down with his left hand and with his right hand he is attempting to stab you. Slash your left hand against his arm at the same time grasping his wrist. Throw him to your left by raising your right leg and hip, hold on to his right wrist and wrap your right arm over his right arm. Apply pressure by clasping your left wrist with your thumb down.

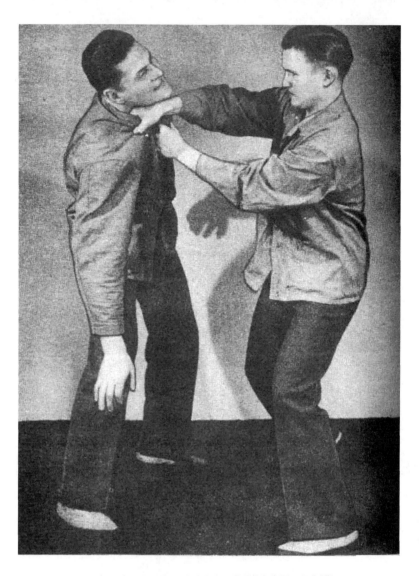

CHOKING WITH COLLAR AND
ARM PRESSURE
(START)

Grasp your opponent's collar just behind the ear with your right hand with your thumb on the outside. At the same time grasp his right lapel with your left hand, pull forward and down with your left hand; and pull back and up with your right hand.

CHOKING WITH COLLAR AND
ARM PRESSURE
(FINISH)

At the same time step slightly toward your opponent's rear from his left side, insert your right foot behind his left. You can thus either continue choking him or throw him on his back. This is a very dangerous choke, use caution.

CHOKING WITH COLLAR, AND
THUMB PRESSURE

Grasp your opponent's collar behind his ears with both hands, forcing your thumb behind his windpipe. Pull him forward and raise your knee into his testicles; or go into circle throw.

Alternative Action: Force him backwards by stepping to his right side. Insert your right leg behind his right leg, forcing him to the ground. Continue to strangle him. Very dangerous.

INWARD TWIST COLLAR CHOKE

Grasp your opponent's collar behind the ears with both hands, thumbs inside of collar. Twist collar inside out, holding tightly. Your thumbs are now outside, and your fingers are facing up. Now pull your hands together in a vise-like manner. This will cause immediate strangulation. For additional punishment, kick with knee in the testicles. Very dangerous.

ARM-HOLD FOR MARCHING
A PRISONER

(Instructions on opposite page)

ARM HOLD FOR MARCHING PRISONER

You are facing in the same direction as your opponent, standing at his right. Insert your left arm between his right arm and right side, and with your left hand raise his right hand towards your shoulder, his palm facing backwards. Apply downward pressure against the back of his hand with both your hands.

CLUB OR STICK DEFENSE

Club or stick defense is a compartively new mode of defense. It is very important to military police and police officers and essential to men in the armed forces especially should they find themselves without weapons.

A short stick about 18 inches long, preferably pointed, can be made into a very dangerous weapon. The stick should be laid alongside of your right hand on the inside. By holding the stick in this position, it will not break.

Three inches of the stick should protrude beyond your fingers. In this position it would be very hard for an opponent or enemy to take the stick away from you as it does not look dangerous held in that position. The most effective way to use the stick when held in the right hand is to step in quickly with the right foot and slash down against the face tearing the face open; or jab the stick into the mouth; or slash it against the throat. Other vulnerable spots are jabbing the heart, stomach and testicles. It also makes an effective weapon agains knife attack.

The following pages should be studied closely.

ILLUSTRATING CLUB OR STICK DEFENSE
FOR M.P. OR POLICE OFFICER

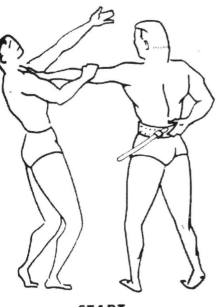

START

FINISH

(Instructions on next Page)

CLUB OR STICK DEFENSE FOR
M. P. OR POLICE OFFICER
START

When enemy attempts to close in on you, hold him back with your left hand and reach back with your right hand. Grasp your club as sketched.

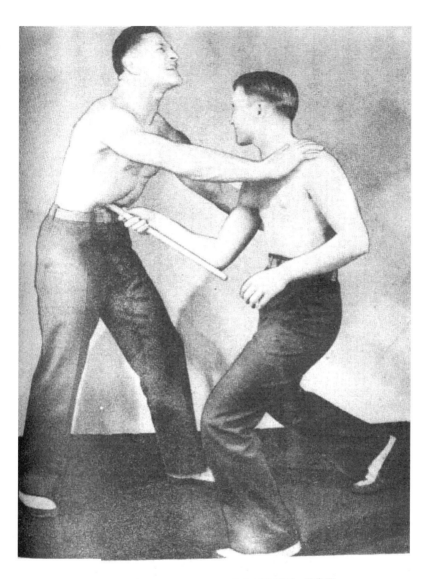

CLUB OR STICK DEFENSE FOR
M. P. OR POLICE OFFICER
FINISH

Jab hard into stomach, heart, neck, mouth, eyes, windpipe; slash against the back or side of neck, against the wrist or jab in the testicles. Use caution in practice.

CLUB OR STICK DEFENSE

(Instructions on opposite Page)

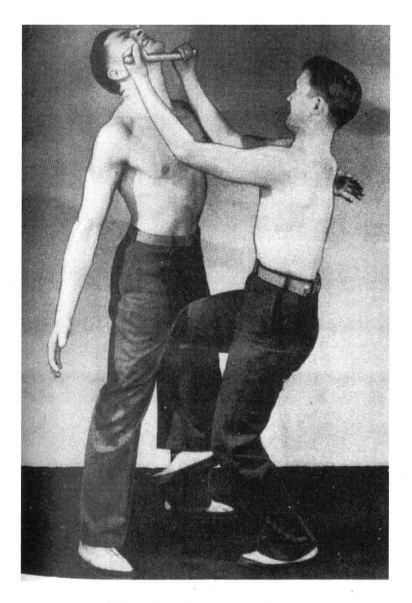

CLUB OR STICK DEFENSE
ACTION AGAINST THROAT

Clasp club or stick with both hands, thumbs up and strike your opponent in neck. Follow up by kicking your knee into testicles. Very effective is blow across the bridge of the nose. It will kill a man instantly.

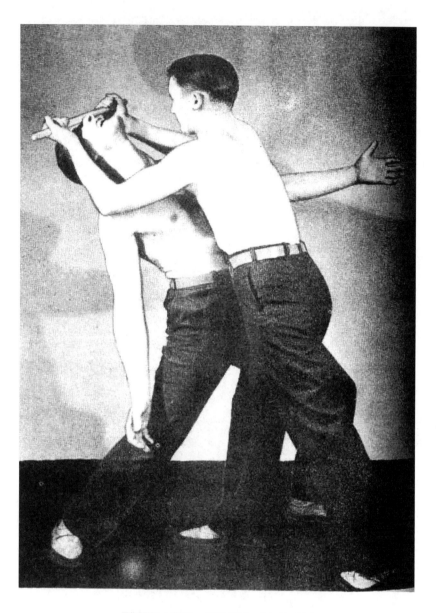

CLUB OR STICK DEFENSE
ACTION AGAINST HEAD

Clasp club or stick with both hands, thumbs up. and
strike your opponent against the forehead or in the
mouth. Use caution in practice.

CLUB OR STICK DEFENSE
AGAINST KNIFE-SLASH FROM THE SIDE

Enemy attempts to slash at you from the side with his right hand. Hold club in your right hand alongside your forearm and drive it against his wrist.

CLUB OR STICK DEFENSE

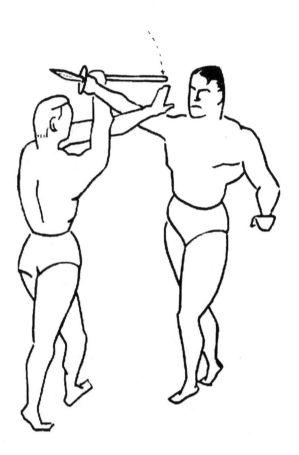

START

Enemy jabs knife down at you. Cross your right hand over your left, while holding your club with your right hand. Receive the knife jab between your crossed hands. Force the club over his forearm towards your crossed left hand at same time grabbing club with your left hand.

CLUB OR STICK DEFENSE

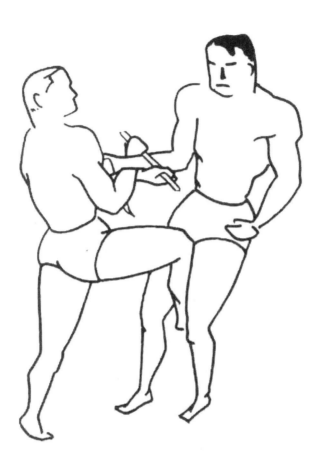

FINISH

Force down on club which will bend him forward. Step into him and kick hard with your knee into his testicles. At the same time pressing down on his forearm which will break it. Use caution in practice.

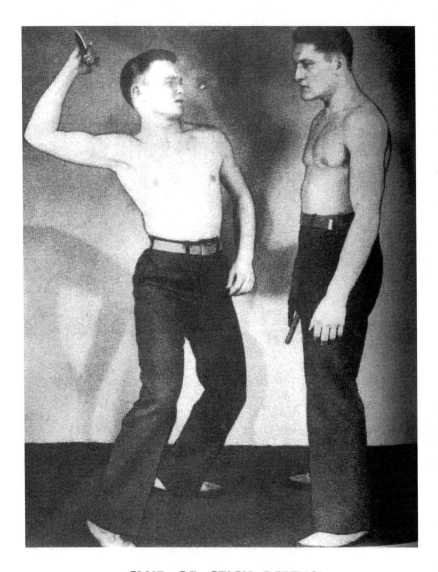

CLUB OR STICK DEFENSI
ACTION AGAINST SHARP WEAPON
ACTION 1

Enemy jabs knife down at you. Do not step back.

CLUB OR STICK DEFENSE
ACTION AGAINST SHARP WEAPON
ACTION 2

Step towards your opponent as you cross your right hand over your left, holding your club in your right hand. Receive the knife jab between your crossed hands. Force the club over his fore-arm towards your crossed left hand and grab the club.

CLUB OR STICK DEFENSE
ACTION AGAINST SHARP WEAPON
FINISH

Force down on the club thus causing him to bend forward. Step towards him and kick hard with your knee in the chin or testicles. Continue pressing down on the forearm, causing it to break. USE CAUTION IN PRACTICE.

CLUB OR STICK DEFENSE

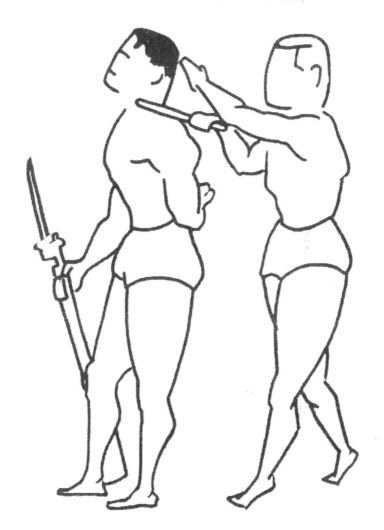

START

Silencing and disarming a sentry. Approach silently then quickly cross your left hand over your right hand which is holding the club. Force the club around his throat. Grasp it quickly with your left hand. Force it against his windpipe crushing it. VERY dangerous in practice.

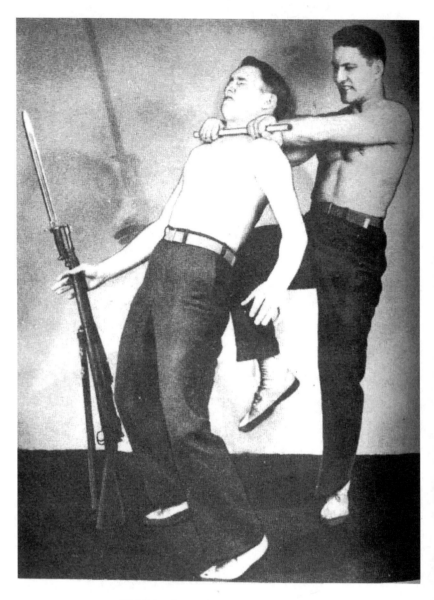

CLUB OR STICK DEFENSE
FINISH

Pull back on club, push knee into his back violently breaking his spine. Force body to ground slowly, holding tightly to stick which will strangle him. Very dangerous to practice. Use Caution.

DISARMING

The following pages will consist of proper methods of disarming the enemy armed with the following weapons:

PISTOL

RIFLE AND BAYONET

MACHETE

KNIFE

CLUB

All of disarming action is very violent and dangerous. Use caution in practice.

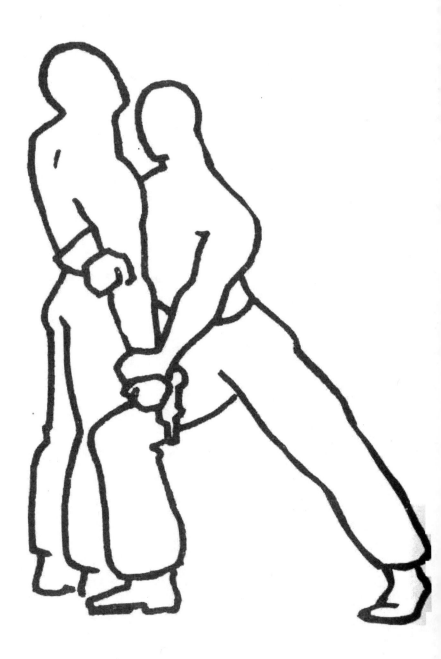

(Instructions on opposite Page)

DISARMING TRICK NO. 1

Your enemy attempts to use weapon from the side:

Grasp his right wrist with your left hand. Step forward with right foot while sliding your right arm between his arm and side. Crook arm forming an "L" clenching fist tightly. Strike back of elbow sharply with center of your forearm. This will cause him considerable pain forcing him to drop his weapon.

If he attempts to throw his free hand about your neck, go into "Over Shoulder Throw."

ILLUSTRATING DISARMING TRICK NO. 2

(Instructions on opposite page)

DISARMING TRICK NO. 2

Your enemy attempts to capture you and holds weapon to your stomach:

Clasp his right hand at the wrist with your left hand (your thumb facing down). At the same time step back with your right foot—180 degrees; holding his arm and pulling slightly while rotating and twisting it palm up towards your body. Lean back and down against his arm clamping your elbow against his arm and holding it tightly to your side.

Disarm by turning gun toward his face with your right hand. Strike him with captured weapon on the back of his neck. Continue holding him by leaning back against his arm.

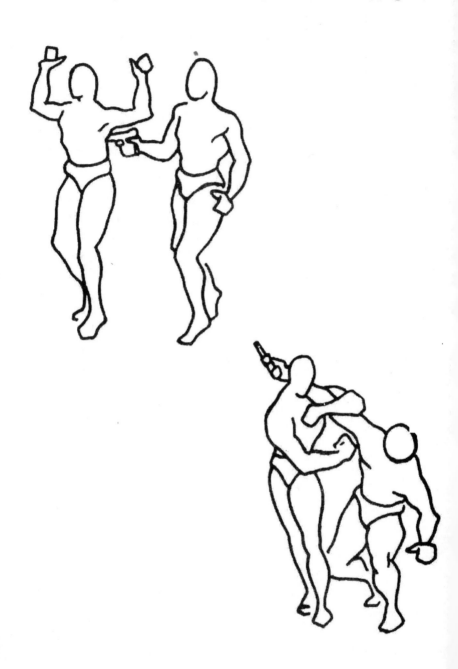

(Instructions on opposite page)

DISARMING TRICK NO. 3

Your enemy attempts to capture you; marching you with weapon in your side. He is one step behind you:

Stop suddenly with right foot forward; sweeping your left hand down along your side and back over his arm in a rotating motion anchoring his hand against your shoulder and neck. Press down hard against his elbow and strike his face with free hand or knee.

Or:

Reach back over your head with your right hand and disarm him. Then hit him in back of neck with weapon.

ILLUSTRATING DEFENSE AGAINST
MACHETE—CLUB—KNIFE

(Instructions on opposite page)

DEFENSE AGAINST
MACHETE—CLUB—KNIFE

Your enemy attempts to strike you across head and shoulders with weapon with his right hand:

Cross hands above your head, right hand in front of left. Receive the blow in the "V" formed by hands. Then grasp his wrist with your right hand rotating his arm towards you so that his hand will face up. At the same time slide your right foot back about 50 degrees. Apply pressure downward on his elbow with your left forearm.

To put enemy out of action force him slowly to ground holding him firmly. Step over his right arm with your left foot and sit on his shoulder and break his arm by pulling up hard.

DEFENSE AGAINST KNIFE, CLUB, MACHETE
START

Your enemy attempts to strike you across head and shoulders with weapon with his right hand:

Cross hands above your head, right hand in front of left. Receive the blow in the "V" formed by hands. Then grasp his wrist with your right hand rotating his arm towards you so that his hand will face up.

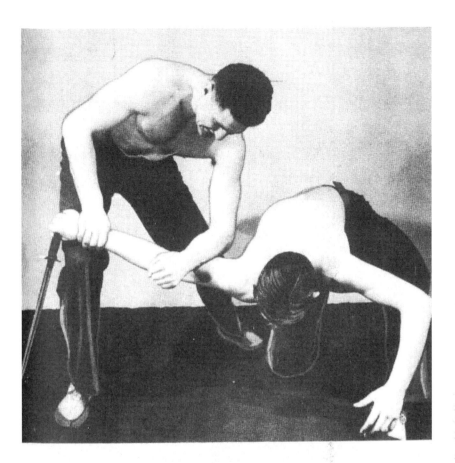

DEFENSE AGAINST KNIFE, CLUB. MACHETE
FINISH

At the same time slide your right foot back about 50 degrees. Apply pressure downward on his elbow with your left forearm.

To put enemy out of action force him slowly to ground holding him firmly. Step over his right arm with your left foot and sit on his shoulder and break his arm by pulling up hard.

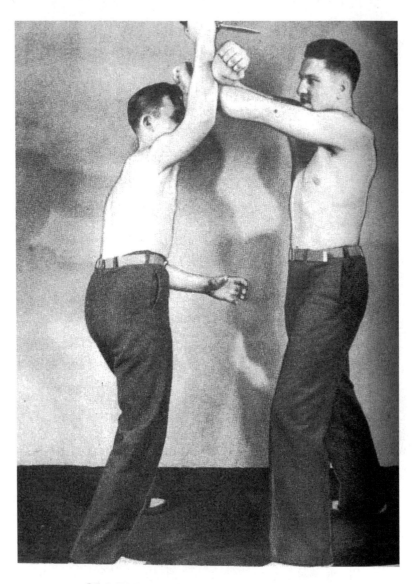

CROSSED ARM BLOCK AGAINST DOWNWARD SLASH WITH ARM-BREAK

START

Enemy attempts to strike you with knife in a downward motion. Cross hands above your head, right hand on top of left. Receive the blow in the "V" formed by your hands.

CROSSED ARM BLOCK AGAINST DOWNWARD SLASH WITH ARM-BREAK FINISH

Force his arm back with your right arm in an "L."

Remove your left hand and insert it in the crook of his right arm. Grasp your own forearm, pressing down with your right and pulling up with your left, thus causing dislocation of his arm.

ARM BREAK, AND OVER-SHOULDER THROW
ACTION 1

Against knife or revolver.

Enemy attempts to use weapon from his hip with his right hand. Step in with your left foot and left hand, grasping his wrist, with your thumb on the inside.

ARM BREAK, AND OVER-SHOULDER THROW
ACTION 2

Against knife or revolver.

Continue holding his right arm, pulling down slightly.
Insert your right arm between his right arm and right
side, forming an "L" with your right arm, forcing it hard
against the crook of his arm and breaking it. Very
dangerous.

ARM BREAK, AND OVER-SHOULDER THROW
FINISH

Against knife or revolver.

Enemy may attempt to throw his left arm around **your** neck. Continue holding his right arm and go into **an** over-shoulder throw.

BAYONET DISARMING

Official U. S. Navy Photograph

You are being attacked by enemy armed with bayonet; He is aiming for your body

Bring your right foot behind you and grasp the muzzle of his rifle with your right hand palm down—your left hand grasps the balance of his rifle palm up. Push up with your left hand and down with your right hand— pushing bayonet into ground. Keep your right foot to the left of bayonet by stepping directly behind him. Pushing him forward violently. This will force him to let go of rifle. You will then be able to attack him with his own rifle.

RIFLE AND BAYONET DISARMING
ACTION NO. 1

Official U. S. Navy Photograph

Enemy attacks you and is pointing bayonet at your body

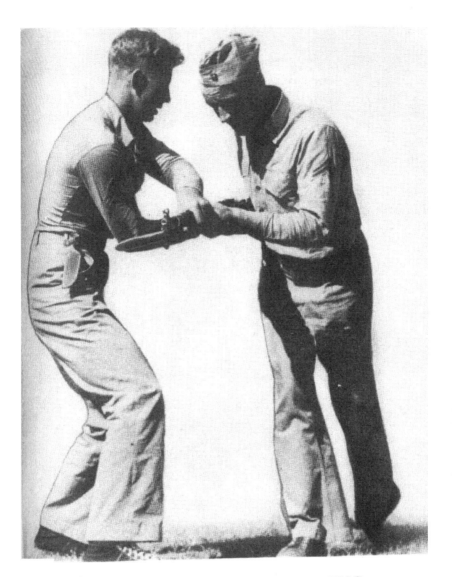

RIFLE AND BAYONET DISARMING
ACTION NO. 2

Official U. S. Navy Photograph

Step or pivot towards your left, grasp rifle in back of the bayonet with your left hand, pulling up and with your right hand grasp the back of the balance of rifle, pulling down.

RIFLE AND BAYONET DISARMING
ACTION NO. 3

Official U. S. Navy Photograph

Take one step back which will force his arm and rifle to point backwards and downwards.

RIFLE AND BAYONET DISARMING
ACTION NO. 4—FINISH

Official U. S. Navy Photograph

Your enemy's forward momentum will force him to let go of rifle. Reverse the same and slash at the back of neck. Use caution in practice.

RIFLE AND BAYONET DISARMING
START

Official U. S. Navy Photograph

At close quarters enemy attempts to drive rifle, held flat, directly in front of him into your face. Cross arms and twist to your left.

RIFLE AND BAYONET DISARMING
FINISH

Official U. S. Navy Photograph

By twisting to your left it will cause him to let go of the rifle. Now reverse rifle and bayonet and attack him. Use caution in practice.

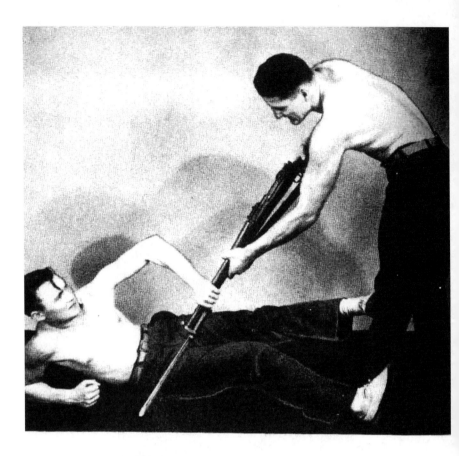

DEFENSE AGAINST BAYONET

If knocked to ground and attacked, hook right foot about
your enemy's ankle, toe in. Pull towards you and push
with other foot against inside of knee joint. Parry bayonet thrust and disarm.

FOX-HOLE TRICK

Coming out of foxhole, clasp enemy's leading foot, using hand on same side. Thrust hard with forearm against inside of knee joint, pushing out and back. Climb across enemy using knee in testicles and choke.
This may be performed with either hand.

THE PURPOSE OF THE COMBAT
CONDITIONING PROGRAM

The purpose of the following activities is for speeding up the physical training of our Marines as well as the youth of the nation.

Many of the instructions are not new as they are the same as have been used in the past. This war has created many new problems and, therefore, speed is essential primarily in combat conditioning. Our program has taken this into consideration by adopting all the new methods for conditioning the men.

A definite time is set for the program. Participation is compulsory. A systematic plan is followed, as outlined in the following pages. Effective administration calls for the cooperation of all officers and men.

COMBAT CONDITIONING
PROGRAM

I. Drill:
1. Manual of Arms (5 minutes).
2. Close and Extended Order (15 minutes).
3. Physical Drill Under Arms (5 minutes).
   Stack Arms (3 minutes).

II. Accelerated Calisthenics—Stress Speed—No Rests.
1. Clap hands—running in place accelerate.
2. Side straddle hop hand slapping head — 16 counts. Rythm — 16 counts — speed — men count.
3. Side straddle hop—hands on deck—16 counts. Rhythm—16 counts—speed—men count.
4. Breathing exercise—
(a) Inhale—hold breath—pound chest with fists. Exhale.
   1. Repeat once.
(b) Inhale—hold breath—hammer stomach with sides of hand—exhale.
   1. Repeat once.
5. Extend arms, touch alternate feet with opposite hand—stretch—2 counts—16 counts—men count.
   (a) Bend extend arms—wind mill—16 counts —speed—men count.
6. Russian dance—arm bend—squat—left leg out —8 counts — right — 8 counts — alternate — 16 counts—latter—fast—shake legs out, at finish.
7. Clasp hands under knees — shuffling feet — alternate 16 counts—rhythm—16 counts—fast.
8. Stoop sitting—hands between legs—left foot back 8 counts—right foot back—8 counts—both back 16 counts.
9. Grass drill—running in place—front go—back go—right go—left go—back go—front go.

10. Push ups—hands under chest—push up both hands and feet off deck—slap hands—catch self—let down—accelerate action.
11. Hands at side—heels six inches off deck—heels and hands out—back—accelerate action. Alternate with heels six inches off deck hammering stomach.
12. Rocking horse.
13. Bicycle exercise.
14. Alternate with rotating feet—stiff legged bringing heels close to ground—also sitting up slowly—back to prone slowly.
15. Heels and toes on deck alternately.
16. Hurdlers' exercise.

UP ON FEET

III. Contact—Pair Off:
1. Hand wrestling.
2. Lock back of necks—bulldogging.
3. Exchange hands on opponent's chest alternating feet.
4. Same except heels of hands in abdomen. Accelerate above.
5. Pushing exercise—drape arm over opponent's neck, one hand on deck—push.
6. Lock arms back to back — pull up — shake opponent.
7. Rooster fighting.
8. Fireman carry.

IV. Tumbling:
1. Forward somersault.
2. Backward somersault—knees high—run backward.
3. Side roll.
   (b) Alternate sides.
4. General warm-ups—on mat—stress recovery with hands up.

V. Hand to Hand Phase:
1. Chokes and breaks.
2. Wrist lock and breaks.
3. Use of helmets—pails—tops of GI cans to keep
4. Hip throw.
5. All judo throws—slams.
6. Breaks for same.
7. Elbows—forearms—offensive use of same.
8. Kicks—stamps.
9. Pistol and knife—disarming.
10. Mass bare handed boxing.

VI. Club Routine.

VII. Bayonet Drill—new.
(b) Disarming.

VIII. Obstacle Course with Rifles and Bayonets.

IX. Rope Climbing.

X. Swimming routine when possible—IV, V, VI, VII, VIII, IX used alternately—stressing V, VI, VIII as troops progress.

NOTE: Swim program should include:
1. Tread water — proper breathing — variety of strokes.
2. Use of trousers—shirts as water wings.
3. Use of helmets—pails—tops of GI cans to keep one afloat.
4. Proper way to leave deck of sinking aircraft carrier or troopship.
5. Methods of swimming in water where oil is aflame.
6. Life saving methods:
   (a) Towing comrade.
   (b) Breaking desperation holds.
7. Resuscitation.

Made in the USA
Columbia, SC
25 September 2024